MAIL RAIL

MAIL RAIL

From beginning to end

A brief history of the Post
Office's underground railway

MIKE SULLIVAN

First published in 2019 by Redshank Books

Redshank Books is an imprint of Libri Publishing.

ISBN 978-1-912969-00-5

A CIP catalogue record for this book is available from
The British Library

Cover and book design by Carnegie Book Production

Printed in the UK by Halstan

Libri Publishing
Brunel House
Volunteer Way
Faringdon
Oxfordshire
SN7 7YR

Tel: +44 (0)845 873 3837

www.libripublishing.co.uk

CONTENTS

Acknowledgements

The production of this book would not have been possible without the encouragement, support and contributions of all my colleagues, both staff and volunteers, at The Postal Museum.

Particular thanks go to Isabelle Reynolds-Logue who volunteered to proof read and edit this volume through its various phases of development.

I would also like to acknowledge the support I have received from my publishers.

The majority of the images used in this volume were provided courtesy of The Postal Museum, and the copyright is held by Royal Mail Group.

Other images are provided by:

The Kempton Steam Museum
The London Transport Museum
The Museum of London
The Postal Museum
John Edser
Peter Johnson

Every effort has been made to establish the provenance of the other images and, if any errors have occurred, please accept my sincerest apologies.

Thank you all

Mike Sullivan

LIST OF ILLUSTRATIONS

The Great East Express
  ©John Edser

Congestion on London Bridge
  ©Museum of London

Post Office Railway Route
  ©Royal Mail Group, Courtesy of The Postal Museum

Greathead Shield
  ©London Transport Museum

Route Maps
  ©Royal Mail Group, Courtesy of The Postal Museum

Proposed Extensions
  ©Royal Mail Group, Courtesy of The Postal Museum

1927 Rolling Stock
  ©Royal Mail Group, Courtesy of The Postal Museum

Evan Evans' Sketch
  ©Royal Mail Group, Courtesy of The Postal Museum

1930s Rolling Stock
  ©John Edser

Diagram of 1980s Bogie Showing Major Components
  ©Royal Mail Group, Courtesy of The Postal Museum

1980s Greenbat Rolling Stock
  ©Royal Mail Group, Courtesy of The Postal Museum

Artist's Drawing of Greenbat Train
  ©Royal Mail Group, Courtesy of The Postal Museum

System Display Screen
©Peter Johnson

Photo of Tipper
©Royal Mail Group, Courtesy of The Postal Museum

Tipper in use at Paddington
©Royal Mail Group, Courtesy of The Postal Museum

Station Schematic
©Royal Mail Group, Courtesy of The Postal Museum

Intertwined Spiral Chutes
©Royal Mail Group, Courtesy of The Postal Museum

Schematic Drawing of Vertical Riser
©Royal Mail Group, Courtesy of The Postal Museum

Conveyors at Paddington
©Royal Mail Group, Courtesy of The Postal Museum

Route Label Board
©Royal Mail Group, Courtesy of The Postal Museum

The New Mail Rail Experience
©The Postal Museum

Mule Used to Establish New Train Dimensions
© The Postal Museum

New Train
©The Postal Museum

En route on the Mail Rail Ride
©The Postal Museum

Transport Heritage Trust Award
©The Postal Museum

The Great East Express on its way from Liverpool Street to Paddington; travel time: 15 minutes (Courtesy of John Edser)

INTRODUCTION

On 5th December 1927 the General Post Office (GPO), as it was then called, celebrated the launch of its parcel service from Mount Pleasant to Paddington on the world's first driverless, electric, underground railway. Between 19th and 24th December a parcel service ran from Mount Pleasant to Liverpool Street for the Christmas pressure period. By 12th March 1928, all stations had been commissioned and a full letter and parcel service, the Post Office Railway (POR), was operating over the full length of the system from Whitechapel to Paddington.

In the early hours of 31st May 2003, the last train ran and the long and distinguished record of speeding mail below the streets of London was over.

An extract from the Post Office archive describing the history of the Post Office Railway between 1854 and 2003 can be found in Appendix 1.

To discover more about this unique and innovative system we should start by asking two questions: why did they build it in the first place, and why did it close?

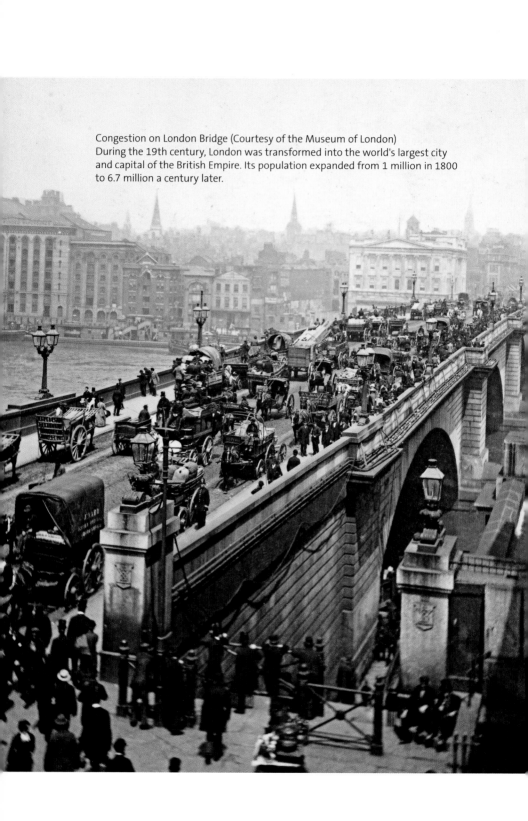

Congestion on London Bridge (Courtesy of the Museum of London)
During the 19th century, London was transformed into the world's largest city
and capital of the British Empire. Its population expanded from 1 million in 1800
to 6.7 million a century later.

THE EARLY DAYS

To answer the first question we have to ask ourselves what London was like at the turn of the century. Not the one just gone, but the one before that. London in the 1890s–1900s was a fast-growing, bustling city. The population had increased from 2.7 million in 1851 to 6.6 million in 1901. The air was often filled with fog or smog as people burned coal or wood either to keep warm or to generate steam for their factory machinery. Street lighting, if any, was predominantly gas lit with the occasional main road being served by the latest innovation: electric light bulbs. The railways were making good progress, particularly the London Underground, which was making use of electric motors to drive the trains and lighting through their tunnels. The London Underground first used a four-rail system in 1890, with two rails giving a 660-volt DC (Direct Current) supply and return for the traction motors, on what was to become part of the Northern Line.

The streets themselves were becoming increasingly congested as trade and commerce expanded at an ever-growing rate. The mode of transport was predominantly horse drawn with 60% being omnibuses and hackney carriages and the remainder being mostly goods vehicles. Youngsters regularly followed behind with their buckets and spades collecting manure for mum's garden or to be sold to the neighbours for a few pence pocket money. The occasional motorised car, van or bus could be seen but the net result of all this activity was an average speed across the centre of town being noted as a sluggish 6mph.

The General Post Office, with its continuing obsession with moving the mail faster from its post boxes to people's letter boxes, and its willingness to experiment and innovate, formed a committee on 30th September 1909 to consider ways in which it could move its increasing volumes of mail underground, below the streets of London.

Robert Bruce, the controller of the London Postal Region at the time, became chairman of the committee with the following objectives.

To consider and report upon:
  a) The relative merits, for the transportation of mails, of the various systems of Pneumatic Tubes and Underground Electric Railways;
  b) The advantages and disadvantages of those systems compared with the present methods of transmitting mails; and
  c) The increase or reduction in expense which might be anticipated if any such system or systems were established on the route or routes in London which are most suitable for the purpose.

The committee initially considered both pneumatic and electric systems but became increasingly inspired by the Chicago Tunnelling Company who had built 60 miles of tunnel under the shopping and commercial centre of Chicago to deliver goods to the shops during the day and remove waste and ash overnight.

The carriages used in Chicago were pulled by locomotives, probably very similar to the three battery locomotives that the Post Office Railway purchased for emergency and maintenance use when the system was powered down. Each of the Chicago locomotives required a driver working in dark and dusty conditions to keep the system operational.

The committee reported back in February 1911 with a detailed proposal to build an underground railway running approximately 70-feet under the streets of London. It would use driverless, electric trains and serve all of the main sorting offices along the six-and-a-half-mile stretch between Whitechapel in the east and Paddington in the west. The system would be a narrow gauge (2-foot) railway with a third rail running down the centre of the track to provide power at 440-volt Direct Current (DC) in the main tunnels and 150-volt DC in the stations.

The standard gauge for railways is 4-foot 8½ inches. It is also known as the Stephenson gauge as it was used for his original 'Rocket'. Robert Stephenson designed the 'Rocket' steam locomotive in 1829 for the Liverpool and Manchester Railway. It is said that this gauge was derived because tooling used to make the wheels and axles was an adaptation of that used to make the wheels of stagecoaches. Stagecoach wheels in turn were made to fit comfortably in the ruts that were commonplace in the roads of the time. These ruts were originally carved out by the chariots that travelled all over the country during the Roman occupation.

Anything less than this standard gauge was known as narrow gauge. The Post Office Railway, with a nominal 2-foot distance between the running rails, was thus a narrow-gauge railway.

The original route of the railway is shown in the following image.

At that time the GPO was a government department staffed by civil servants and was either being financed by or making a contribution to the Treasury. The proposal for a new railway was placed before the British Parliament in November 1912 and on 15th August 1913 the Post Office Railway (London) Act 1913 received royal assent, allowing construction to commence with a budget of 1.1 million pounds.

An important stipulation in the Act was that it was expressly forbidden for this new railway to carry passengers, thus avoiding any conflict of interest with London Underground or any other privately owned transportation company.

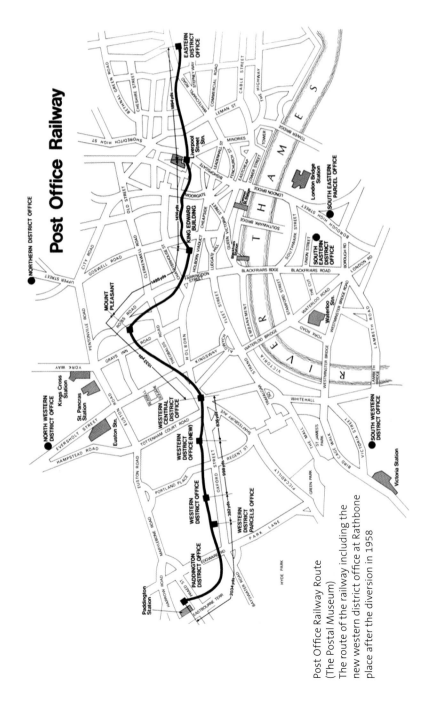

Post Office Railway Route
(The Postal Museum)
The route of the railway including the
new western district office at Rathbone
place after the diversion in 1958

Tunnelling commenced in October 1914 with an expectation that all the work would be completed and the system would become operational within 15 months. Sadly the commencement of the First World War had a significant impact on the timetable.

Greathead Shield (Courtesy of London Transport Museum)
Tunnelling shields allowed deep tunnels to be driven through soft earth instead of being dug as trenches and then covered up. The shield protected workers cutting the earth at the tunnelling face. It slowly moved forward, with the tunnel being lined behind it to ensure that it didn't collapse. They were the forerunners of the modern giant tunnelling machines used to dig the Channel Tunnel and the soon-to-open Elizabeth Line.
Adapted from British Library Science blog 19th December 2017

THE TUNNELS

The tunnels were hand dug using a 'Greathead Shield' to protect the excavation from collapsing. A Greathead Shield is like a giant pastry cutter that is driven into the soft earth, predominantly London Clay, to support the surrounding ground while the earth within the shield is removed by hand. A ring of cast-iron segments is then added to the existing tunnel before driving the shield forward again to continue the process. The tunnel segments were 20-inches wide, so every time this cycle was completed, the tunnel moved further forward towards its destination.

The first shield was designed by the father of Isambard Kingdom Brunel, Marc Brunel, and was rectangular in shape, supporting the earth while tunnelling progressed. The shield was used to build the Thames Tunnel between Wapping and Rotherhithe, the world's first tunnel to be built under water. It opened in 1869 and almost 150 years later is still in daily use as part of the London Overground network.

Other engineers made various improvements over time, the most notable design being the aforementioned shield of James Henry Greathead. His design, which he used extensively when tunnelling new London Underground tube lines, was circular, allowing the load to be spread more evenly. This became the system of choice and was the basis of future mechanised systems that are used today. It was his design that earned the London Underground the nickname 'The Tube.'

The contract for the construction of the tunnels was given to John Mowlem on 27th November 1914, with the expectation that the work would be completed in 15 months. The first shaft was dug in the Paddington Basin. Seven other shafts were dug on the route with tunnelling taking place in both directions. When the tunnels met underground the maximum discrepancy was one-eighth of an inch.

The declaration of war with Germany in 1914 prompted a major re-think by the government on the funding of this project. The decision was made to complete the tunnels but place on hold any further expenditure until a later date. Even then, with large numbers of able-bodied men going off to war and the scarcity of raw materials due to their diversion to the war effort, tunnelling was not completed until 1917.

The construction of the railway was fraught with difficulties. On 8th and 9th of April 1915, water from the adjacent River Fleet found its way into the tunnel just outside of Mount Pleasant. Attempts to shore it up with boarding were unsuccessful and when the water came gushing in, 10 miners had to run for their lives. A 20-foot hole in the roadway was pumped out and the road repaired.

The tunnels that had been completed were put to good use for storing valuable artefacts from the British Museum (including the Rosetta Stone), the Tate Gallery, the National Portrait Gallery, the Wallace Collection and the Public Record Office (now The National Archives) to protect them from Zeppelin bombing raids until the war was over. 9-foot tunnels were finally completed between stations that would allow two narrow-gauge tracks, one in each direction that would then split into two 7-foot tunnels and inclines to slow the trains down on approach and accelerate them on departure. Two tunnels with large platforms formed the station area, one for the eastbound traffic and one for westbound, with connecting cross tunnels between the two platforms. The stations varied in length: the shortest at the Western District Office was 90-foot and the longest at Mount Pleasant was 313-foot. The station tunnels at Mount Pleasant and King Edward Building were 25-foot in diameter. All of the other stations had a tunnel diameter of 21-foot 2½ inches.

Fairly early in the process a future extension from King Edward Building was proposed to link up with London Bridge, Waterloo, and Victoria, returning to the Western Central office in Holborn. Further extensions to the Northern District office and a loop serving Kings Cross, St Pancras, the North Western District office and Euston were also proposed. Some years later, when British Rail were building a new freight depot at Willesden that would also be a terminus for travelling post offices, an extension from Paddington to Willesden was also proposed.

These extensions were all considered by the Post Office board, but since the cost of tunnelling had increased significantly after the war years to more than a million pounds per mile, none were considered to be financially viable and no additional building work took place.

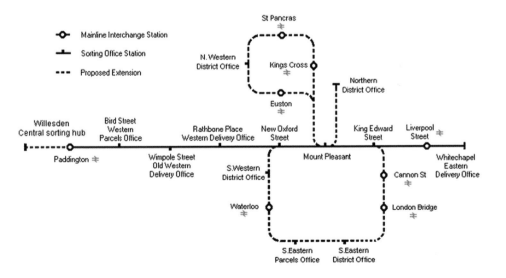

Proposed Extensions (The Postal Museum)
Diagram showing the proposed extensions to the railway; the decision was made to build the main route and consider the extensions at a later date. None of the extensions were ever built.

THE POST OFFICE RAILWAY

(NOT TO SCALE)

PADDINGTON

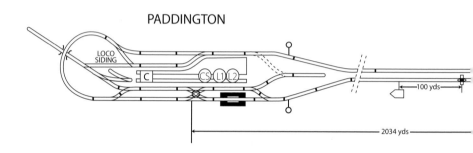

WESTERN DISTRICT OFFICE (R.P)

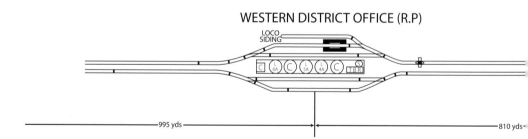

C	CABIN	Ⓢ	STAIRS	Ⓛ1	LIFT (No1 etc.)	ⓈH	SKIP HOIST
Ⓒ	CHUTE	ⒸⓈ	CHUTE & STAIRS	Ⓑ	BAG ELEVATOR	ⓋR	VERTICAL RISER

Route Maps showing station track
layouts (The Postal Museum)

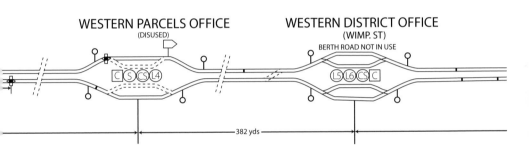

WESTERN PARCELS OFFICE
(DISUSED)

WESTERN DISTRICT OFFICE
(WIMP. ST)
BERTH ROAD NOT IN USE

C S CS L4

L5 L6 CS C

382 yds

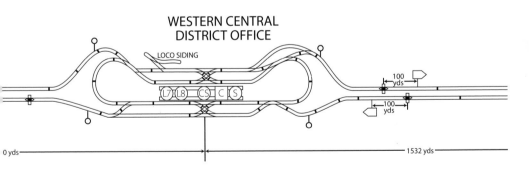

WESTERN CENTRAL
DISTRICT OFFICE

LOCO SIDING

L7 L8 CS C S

100 yds

100 yds

0 yds

1532 yds

| T B R | TWIN BAND RISER | ⚲ | STATION STOP BOARD | ------- | FORMER CONNECTIONS NOW REMOVED |
| ▬ | SUB STATION | ◁ | WRONG ROAD SHUNT BOARD | ⊕ | DIVIDING LINE BETWEEN TWO STATIONS SUPPLY |

THE POST OFFICE RAILWAY

(NOT TO SCALE)

MOUNT PLEASANT

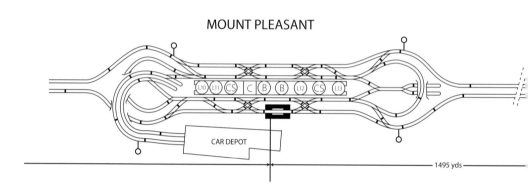

CAR DEPOT

1495 yds

LIVERPOOL STREET

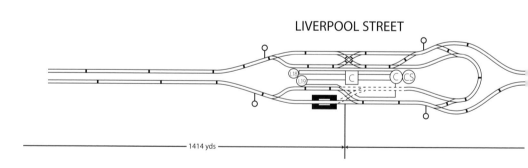

1414 yds

C CABIN	S STAIRS	L1 LIFT (No1 etc.)	SH SKIP HOIST
C CHUTE	CS CHUTE & STAIRS	B BAG ELEVATOR	VR VERTICAL RISER

KING EDWARD BUILDING

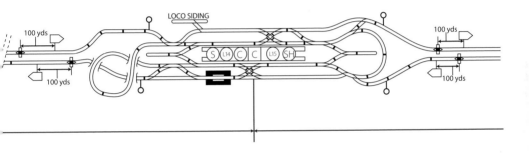

EASTERN DISTRICT OFFICE

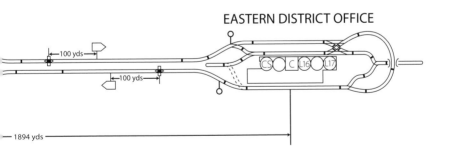

TBR **TWIN BAND RISER**	⚲ **STATION STOP BOARD**	- - - - - - **FORMER CONNECTIONS NOW REMOVED**
▬ **SUB STATION**	⌐ **WRONG ROAD SHUNT BOARD**	⊕ **DIVIDING LINE BETWEEN TWO STATIONS SUPPLY**

The high cost of materials after the war meant that track laying did not start until June 1924 and was not completed until 1927. In total the 6.44 miles between Paddington and Whitechapel were laid with more than 22 miles of track. In 1925 work began on installing the electrical equipment, lifts, conveyors and mail chutes.

The official opening took place at Paddington on 3rd December 1927 when the wife of the London Postal region director, Mrs Gardner, pulled a lever and sent the first train on its way. The system was fully commissioned and operational by March 1928.

During the Second World War, with large numbers of men being called up for military service and a limited railway service operating, the POR platforms were utilised as dormitories and air raid shelters for those required to work in the sorting offices above.

Early in the 1950s the GPO realised that in order to take advantage of the advancements taking place regarding postal mechanisation, with new letter and parcel sorting machines being developed, the majority of existing sorting offices in London and other cities throughout the United Kingdom would not be large enough to accommodate such machinery. Restricted road access and parking at some of the smaller offices also meant that any increase in traffic would cause significant congestion, particularly at the Western District Office and Western Parcels Office. In 1952 the GPO purchased a site in Rathbone Place, just off of Oxford Street and close to Tottenham Court Road, sufficiently large enough to house such machinery and cope with the volume of mail from the Western District Office and the Western Parcels Office combined.

This new office would require a deviation in the original route of the railway. The trains were diverted onto the new track in 1958 with the work required to cut into the existing tunnels and re-route trains onto the new section taking place over six consecutive weekends with no interruption to normal service. Shortly afterwards, the Western District Office and Western Parcels Office were closed with the trains passing through the stations without stopping. The New Western District Office was opened on 3rd August 1965 by Tony Benn, the Postmaster General of the day.

1927 Rolling Stock (The Postal Museum)
The unit had a central compartment for one large container and two smaller trolleys, one over each motor. Two or three units were coupled together to form a train.

THE TRAINS

In 1927 English Electric delivered 90 units that formed the rolling stock for the start of the Post Office Railway service. Two or three of these units were coupled together to form a train, and these trains began carrying mail when the service started in December 1927.

During initial trials the time taken to remove bags of mail from the train and reload it was found to be slowing the operation down. As a result, a wheeled container was designed for placing mail into the central compartment. The containers were made of an aluminium alloy with a canvas cover that stopped items falling out during transit.

Each one was fitted with a flap at the bottom, operated by a foot pedal, so that when the container was placed over a hatch in the platform, the flap could be released to drop the mailbags onto a conveyor and transported up to the sorting office above.

Over time these containers became distorted and difficult to push into the train. Eventually the lower flap was removed so the mailbags had to be removed by hand or emptied by a tipper mechanism.

Even before the service began, one man realised that there would be problems with these trains. Evan Evans was employed by the GPO in 1925 to oversee the completion of the system and become the first manager of the railway. He suggested that the long fixed wheelbase (seven-foot and three inches) between traction units would cause excessive wear on both the tyres on the wheels and the track itself when navigating the tight curves on the system. He sketched a proposal for an articulated train with a traction unit at each end.

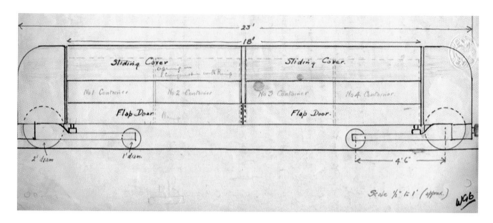

Evan Evans' sketch (The Postal Museum)

His suggestion was dismissed and the 1927 units, of which there were 90, were put into service. However it very quickly became apparent that his reservations about the wear and tear were well founded, and by 1930 a completely new design based on Evans' sketch was introduced. There was a reversible traction unit at each end with an articulated unit that could swivel on pins known as 'king pins' on the drive unit. The centre section could accommodate four large containers and the overall carrying capacity was considerably greater than the 1927 stock.

1930s Rolling Stock (Courtesy of John Edser)
The 1930s stock could carry four large containers and added a reversing switch.

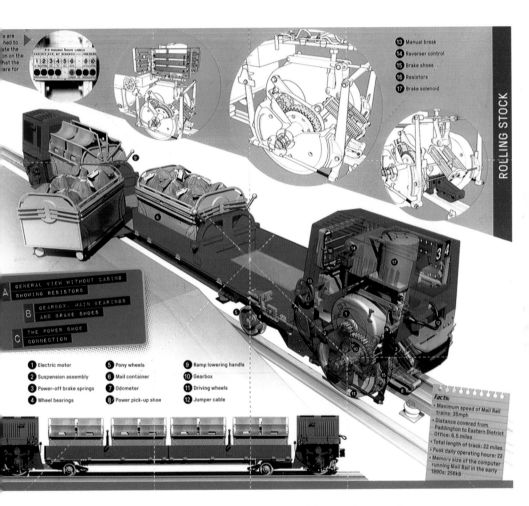

Diagram of 1980s bogie showing major components (The Postal Museum)

The new stock was also built by English Electric and owing to their larger capacity (each container could carry six bags of parcels or 15 bags of letters) and the anticipated traffic, only 50 would be required. They were delivered in two batches, the first in 1930 and the second in 1931. The drive units utilised a lot of the original components from the 1927 stock. This new design was not an immediate success. The pony wheels, the two small twelve-inch wheels behind the drive wheels, had a nasty habit of jumping off the tracks as they passed over points and crossings and around tight bends. After moving the position of the pivot pins to more evenly distribute the weight of the containers the problem was resolved and this new design remained reliably in service until the closure of the railway in May 2003.

In 1936, to increase the capacity of the system, a further 10 units were introduced.

Two collector shoes, one at the front and one at the rear of the bogie pick up the supply to the train. This then goes to a reversing switch that determines the direction of the train. The circuit then passes through the resistors before being fed to the brake solenoid and motor. The current then passes through the axles and wheels back to one of the running rails that is connected to earth along its length.

The reversing switch has a notch in the neutral position that allows a lever to be lifted and the brake, which is held on by spring pressure, to be wound off so that the train may be pushed by hand or towed by a locomotive.

When the train is stationary, the motor has a very low resistance that would draw an extremely large current from the supply when starting. The resistors reduce this current to a manageable level and also avoid complications when one shoe is on the 440-volt supply and the other is on the 150-volt supply.

The brake solenoid is a large electromagnet that lifts the brakes off so that the train can proceed. The brakes are normally held on by large springs so that if the supply to the train is lost the brakes will come on and stop the train.

The motor is a 22-horsepower series wound motor that will give maximum torque for moving the train from a stationary position. As the speed of the motor increases, the amount of current required to propel the train is considerably reduced.

The trains ran for 22 hours a day, six days a week with a shutdown period for minor maintenance and repairs between 08:00 and 10:00 each weekday morning. The system also shut down from 22:00 on a Saturday evening until 10:00 Monday morning to allow for larger works and regular cleaning to be carried out.

Two new prototype trains were introduced in 1962. The design was fundamentally the same as the 1930s stock, but used updated components including disc brakes, new resistors, a new loading ramp system and new motors that would provide better acceleration. These modifications would increase the time between servicing, and the trains were more streamlined to improve their efficiency.

These prototypes were tested extensively and formed the basis of the 'Greenbat' stock that was introduced between 1980 and 1982. The original Greenbat trains were being manufactured by Greenwood and Batley who sadly went into administration in April 1980. The company was bought by the Hunslet Holdings Company who retained the name for the new stock. 34 new trains were built and ran alongside the original trains until the end of the service.

In 1986 three units were fitted with aerodynamic covers designed to reduce drag while providing sufficient cooling for the resistors.

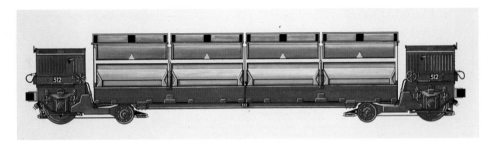

Artist's drawing of Greenbat train (The Postal Museum)

1980s Greenbat Rolling Stock (The Postal Museum)
The Greenbat train is fundamentally the same design as the 1930s stock but with updated components.

English Electric also supplied three battery-operated locomotives in 1927 at a cost of £1,476 pounds each. These were stationed at King Edward Building, Mount Pleasant, and Paddington. They were used in the event of a breakdown and the loco at Mount Pleasant was also used to deliver spares and

Loading a streamlined Greenbat train (The Postal Museum)
The flap, flush with the platform, meant that containers were easy to slide on and off the train. It also secured the containers while in transit.

Streamlined Greenbat (Courtesy of John Edser)
Three units were fitted with additional streamlining that reduced drag and improved the air flow to cool the resistors.

sometimes people during the two-hour shutdown period that occurred each day for minor maintenance. One day it would go to Paddington and back and the next day it would go to Whitechapel and back. These locos were rotated every few months to even out the usage and to allow for maintenance to be carried out on the locos themselves. The loco was driven by two 25-horsepower motors from two large battery banks providing 340-volt DC. Increasing the speed control lever in an anti-clockwise direction applied the battery power to the motor in seven stages to give an ever-increasing speed. Returning the lever back to the neutral position and then in a clockwise direction removed the power and placed a resistance across the motor causing it to slow down. This was known as 'dynamic braking.' When the loco was stationary a mechanical brake was screwed on to the wheels to prevent it from rolling away. These locos were capable of towing two fully loaded trains around the entire system on one charge of the batteries. This meant that wherever there was a problem train, it could always be towed back to the car depot. These three locos remained in operation during the life of the railway.

Mail Rail

Battery Operated Recovery Locomotive (The Postal Museum)
The battery locomotives were capable of towing two fully
loaded trains all of the way around the system.

Battery Locomotive Driver's Cabin
(The Postal Museum)

The trains were serviced every 4,000 miles, approximately every ten days, with an inspection and replacement where necessary of all the moving parts, checking and repairing any damage and generally making sure that the train would operate as required. Every 100,000 miles, or every two years, the trains received a more comprehensive strip down and overhaul.

The maintenance work was undertaken in the 'Car Depot', a fully equipped workshop at basement level in Mount Pleasant. It was approached from the main station by a steeply inclined 2-track, 9-foot tunnel.

For safety reasons the power to the trains was supplied by an overhead trolley wire system with a floating power lead that was plugged into the train. An operator on the high-level platform would control the speed of the train while an engineer escorted the train and threw the points by hand where necessary using

Car Depot (The Postal Museum)
Engineers in the car depot could manufacture almost any spare part that was required from raw materials.

sunken operating levers to move the train to the required location.

As well as maintenance stations with an inspection pit for checking underneath the trains, the depot was equipped with a machine shop. This held lathes, milling, grinding, and drilling machines that allowed, if required, almost any part to be manufactured from raw materials. There was also a fully enclosed welding bay and an electric motor overhaul area with a motor test bed where the motors and axles were run for up to a week to ensure their smooth operation.

Occasionally it was desirable to turn around the running rails in the tunnels to even out the wear on them. The only place large enough to do this was the car depot and the battery loco would bring the rails up to the depot where they were manually turned round before being returned to the tunnels.

In 1987, to coincide with the 60th anniversary of the opening of the Post Office Railway, the system was rebranded as 'Mail Rail,' which is how it continues to be referred to today. The rolling stock was repainted red and the stations were given a makeover and new signage to compliment the updated image that Mail Rail would bring.

During the life of the railway, the trains proved to be extremely reliable with very few breakdowns and even fewer collisions. Collisions that did occur were invariably caused by human error. Below is a summary of a story told by Ray Middlesworth, an engineer on the railway for 27 years, about a collision on one eventful day:

> A train must have been going slightly too fast as it approached Mount Pleasant from West Central District Office. It accelerated downhill physically below Theobalds Road before going around a bend in the tunnel at the bottom of the hill. The train leaned to one side and came to rest on the

tunnel wall. Because the wheels were no longer touching both rails the system did not show that this section of track was occupied. The engineer, believing the section to be clear, reset the control circuit. The next train along continued onto this section and ploughed into the rear of the stationary train. The resulting debris from the collision spread onto the adjacent track and in the meantime a train coming in the opposite direction derailed on the debris and now we had three trains piled up like spaghetti.

A list of all the Rolling stock used on the railway can be found in Appendix 2.

Rotary Converter (The Postal Museum)
The rotary converter used mains electricity
to generate the voltages required to run
the railway.

THE SYSTEM

In the 1920s and 1930s railways were continuing to expand and improve throughout the United Kingdom. They soon became the method of choice for transporting Her Majesty's mail across the country.

With Liverpool Street serving Essex and East Anglia, Paddington serving all places west, Mount Pleasant only a short distance away from Kings Cross, Euston and St Pancras serving the north, the Post Office Railway was ideally placed to form the hub of the postal distribution system.

When the system first opened it was supplied with electricity by privately owned companies at 6,600-volt AC (alternating current). This was transformed down and used to drive a rotary converter. A rotary converter is an electric motor driven by the AC supply that drives a DC generator supplying the 440-volt DC or the 150-volt DC to power the trains through the tunnels and the station.

When the electricity companies were nationalised and the National Grid became the source of supply, it arrived at the railway at 11,000-volt. New transformers stepped the voltage down to that required for the rotary converters.

Over time the rotary converters were replaced by more efficient mercury-arc rectifiers. These were large, glass, vacuum-sealed containers with six octopus-like tentacles connected to the AC supply. The arc was like a lightning bolt continuously weaving between the tentacles and a pool of mercury at the bottom of the vessel with an electrical connection giving the positive DC supply.

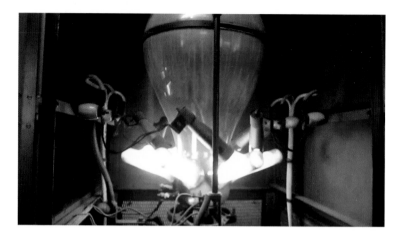

Mercury Arc Rectifier (Courtesy of Kemptonsteam.org)
Mercury arc rectifiers were more efficient and replaced the rotary converters.

Eventually these mercury-arc rectifiers were replaced by even more efficient and reliable solid-state rectifiers.

The DC supply at 440-volt or 150-volt was then supplied to the trains by a third rail running down the centre of the track between the two running rails and three inches higher than the running rails.

Since the system was going to be driverless and fully automatic it was thought to have been nice to make sure that the trains would not bump into each other. Herbert Gunton, who became Principal Power Engineer for the whole of the GPO in 1909, was ideally suited to design the control system. He was born in Manchester in 1874 and was experienced in providing electricity to railways in Manchester, London, and Dublin. The system was designed as a 'fail safe' system where two relays (there were no computers or electronics in those days) were used to provide a positive indication that a train was either occupying a section of the track or that the section was definitely clear. If the section was occupied it would also ensure that the section behind the train was 'dead,' and that if a second train moved onto that section it would stop. The two relays were known as the Stick and the Track relays.

On 29th June 1914 the General Post Office was granted a patent for its innovative design of the control system for driverless trains. It covered route setting and interlocking in stations, braking sections and the use of a dead section behind the train. Phil Sutton, a Technical Officer on the railway in the 1960s and 1970s, gave the following description:

> The two relays were called the Stick and Track relays. The origin of the Stick relay came from the days when trains going in opposite directions used a single track. To avoid the inevitable collisions, one driver would be given a stick which gave him permission to use the track. The stick would then be passed to the driver coming in the opposite direction. If they didn't have the stick, they could not use the track – simple but very effective. And thus the function of the Stick relay was to allow only one train on a piece of track at any one time. The Stick relay, when energised, proved that the section was clear. The Track relay proved it was occupied.

Three Rail track system showing live centre rail (The Postal Museum)
The running rails weighed 35 pounds per yard. The centre conductor rail, mounted three inches higher than the running rails, weighed 15 pounds per yard.

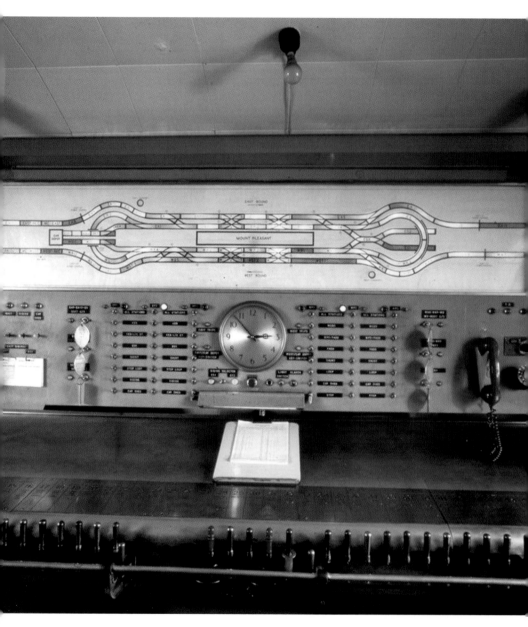

Mount Pleasant switch frame (The Postal Museum)
The switch frame would check the route, throw the points, and apply power to the train. It was designed by Herbert Gunton and the General Post Office was granted patents for its design.

THE OPERATIONS

Driverless trains were running approximately every four minutes with a train being unloaded and reloaded in less than a minute. At its peak the system was carrying over four million letters a day. The journey time from Whitechapel to Paddington if the train stopped at every station was 26 minutes. Non-stopping express trains took only 15 minutes. This reduced the journey time to at least one-third or one-quarter of that taken by road above ground. Trains would run in the main tunnels between stations at about 30 to 35 miles per hour driven by two 440-volt, 22 horsepower DC motors supplied from a third rail running down the centre of the track. On approaching the station, the train would climb an incline and stop. A mechanism would then start the train off at 440-volts and switch the power over to 150-volts to bring the train into the station at about 8 miles per hour, finishing with a controlled stop on the platform. On exit from the station the train would go down an incline, accelerating it on its way to the next station. The mechanism for bringing the trains into the station was replaced by electronic timers. The first was in 1964 and others over time until 1978.

A typical sequence would be to bring the train in to the letters section of the platform, move the train forward to the parcels section of the platform before sending it on its way to the next station. Movements in each station were determined by a controller using a switch frame.

The controller would know the position of all the trains by looking at an illuminated track diagram above the switch frame. To move a train he would pull a lever on the switch frame, moving the train to the desired location. Using this lever was

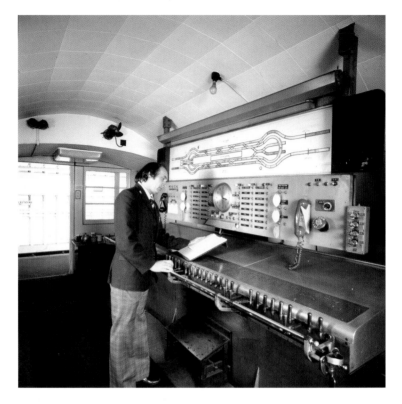

Operator at the Mount Pleasant switch frame (The Postal Museum)

normally a three-position operation. Pulling the lever to the first position caused the control system to check that the track ahead was clear, if it was, a catch was released in the switch frame that allowed the lever to be pulled to the second position. Here the system would check that the points were in the right position, if not the system would throw the points and check again. On the release of the catch the lever could be moved to the third position where power could be applied to the train, moving it on. If the train was on a loading platform, the system would also require the operator loading the train to push a button above his head indicating that the train was ready to depart. This would illuminate a red light known as the 'cherry' warning his colleagues not to approach the train.

Operating the 'Cherry' (The Postal Museum)
A button above the platform, the 'cherry', was pushed to indicate that the train was ready to depart.

This amazing relay-operated control system was once again designed by the Principal Electrical Engineer Herbert Gunton. The original relays, that were open to dust and contamination, were replaced in the 1960s by fully enclosed plug-in relays that were more reliable and required much less maintenance. They remained in use until the closure of the system.

In 1993 a centralised computer-controlled system was opened in Mount Pleasant with a display showing the whole network and being manned by three controllers working shifts. The system communicated with a computer at each station that interfaced with the original control systems. The programme for operating the system was stored in just 256-kilobytes of memory.

Mail Rail

The Vaughan Computer System (Courtesy of Peter Johnson)
The new computer system only used 256 kilobytes of memory.

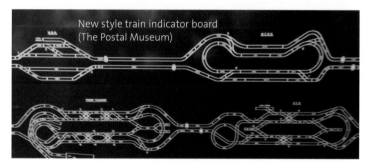

New style train indicator board (The Postal Museum)

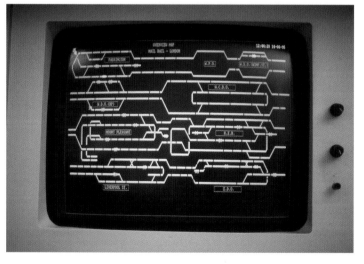

System display screen (Courtesy of Peter Johnson)
Computer screen showing the position of all the trains; this system was introduced in 1993.

The new computer system was installed at the rate of one station per week with no interruption to normal service.

There were two other levers on the switch frame that were used in exceptional circumstances. These were the King Levers, one for each direction, that were used to disconnect the power supply to the tracks in an emergency or when the locomotive was being used.

Pulling the King Lever would allow a key to be removed that ensured that the electricity was off while someone was on the tracks or it was required to operate the points and allow the loco to come out from the sidings. Although power is disconnected the switch frame could still be used to change the points so that the route of the loco could be set up.

At peak times a train would arrive every four minutes and be unloaded and reloaded in less than a minute. Between trains the operators would have to sort bags into the correct containers for dispatch and either tip the containers of incoming mail onto a conveyor feeding a bag elevator or vertical riser, or take the containers to the lift to send upstairs.

Early photograph of tipper
(The Postal Museum)

Tipper in use at Paddington in the 1980s (The Postal Museum)
The tipper was counterbalanced to allow easy discharge of the mailbags

Getting the mail down to the platform from the sorting office above was fairly easy as we had gravity on our side. A pair of intertwined spiral chutes, one to the eastbound platform and one to the westbound normally fed a small conveyor bringing the mailbags out to the respective platform. Getting the mail back up was a little more complex and normally involved wheeling the container into a counterbalanced tipping device that fed a bag elevator or vertical riser. The following sketch is a cut away diagram of a station with an office above showing the spiral chutes and a bag elevator.

At the smaller stations the containers were transported up and down in a goods lift and transferred to and from wicker trolleys in the basement of the sorting office before continuing their journey.

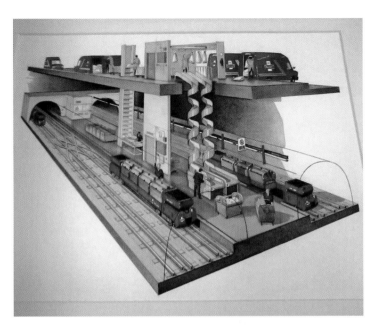

Station schematic
(The Postal
Museum).
Artist's impression
showing chutes and
vertical riser
between the
platforms and
loading bay.

Intertwined spiral
chutes (The Postal
Museum)

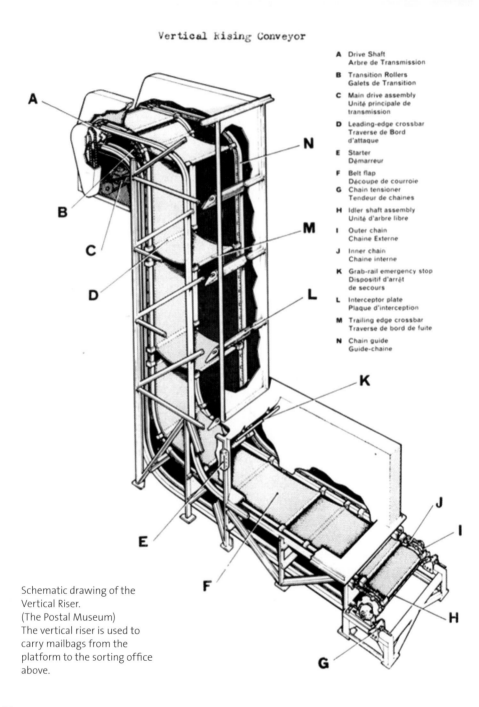

Vertical Rising Conveyor

A Drive Shaft
   Arbre de Transmission
B Transition Rollers
   Galets de Transition
C Main drive assembly
   Unité principale de
   transmission
D Leading-edge crossbar
   Traverse de Bord
   d'attaque
E Starter
   Démarreur
F Belt flap
   Découpe de courroie
G Chain tensioner
   Tendeur de chaines
H Idler shaft assembly
   Unité d'arbre libre
I Outer chain
   Chaine Externe
J Inner chain
   Chaine interne
K Grab-rail emergency stop
   Dispositif d'arrèt
   de secours
L Interceptor plate
   Plaque d'interception
M Trailing edge crossbar
   Traverse de bord de fuite
N Chain guide
   Guide-chaine

Schematic drawing of the
Vertical Riser.
(The Postal Museum)
The vertical riser is used to
carry mailbags from the
platform to the sorting office
above.

Gordon Goddard tells the story of moving the containers at the Western Parcels Office:

> My earliest days as a postman in Western Parcels Office, Bird Street, W1 (next door to Selfridges) I was working nights. The railway lift only reached the basement so there were two of us in the big deserted basement, which was reputed to be haunted all night. Our job was to take the containers off the lift and transfer the bags to the big wicker baskets and put these onto the lift that went up to the sorting office. The latter lift was operated hydraulically by high-pressure water. The water was supplied at high pressure by the Greater London Council via underground pipes. You had to pull the rope in the corner of the lift down to go up and up to go down and catch it just right to stop at the desired floor. Good old days!

At Paddington the mailbags were transported up to the main line station on 390-foot conveyors.

Conveyors at Paddington
(The Postal Museum)
These conveyors ran 390 feet
from the platform at Paddington
to the main line station

P. O. RAILWAY ROUTE LABELS.

E.D.O.	LIV. Sᵀ	K.E.B.	M.P.	W.C.D.O.	W.D.O. (RATHBONE PL.)		PADD.	B.R./W.R.
1	2	3	4	5	6	–	8	10
LETTERS	LETTERS	E.C.	I.S.	W.C.	W.D.O.		LETTERS	LETTERS
1	2	3	4	–	6	6	8	10
PARCELS	PARCELS	F.S.	P.S.		TRANSFERS	P.S.	PARCELS	PARCELS

Route label board (The Postal Museum)
Labels were tied on to each mailbag to show its destination.
White labels indicated letter mail, blue labels parcels.

To determine the destination of each mailbag a hexagonal label with a number on it was attached alongside the normal label. Bags with the same number were put into one container and an identical label was put onto the container.

The number on the destination label determined where the container was removed from the train.
1. Eastern District Office (Whitechapel)
2. Liverpool Street Station
3. Eastern Central District Office (King Edward Building)
4. Mount Pleasant
5. West Central District Office
6. Western District Office (Rathbone Place)
7. Western Parcels Office (closed)
8. Paddington Sorting Office
10. Paddington Mainline Station

A white label was used for letter bags and a blue label for parcels.

There is no number nine label as this could easily be placed upside down and confused with a number six.

THE CLOSURE

The way we communicate and the way we travel has changed dramatically since the railway was first envisaged when the bill was passed in 1913. Hand-writing letters and sending them in the post is a dying art, long since overtaken by email, text messaging, Facebook, Twitter, WhatsApp, Skype and a plethora of other applications that we now access using the computers we carry in our pockets.

Our letter box in now mainly for bills, the latest offers from companies vying for our cash and the occasional packet from eBay or Amazon.

Advances in postal mechanisation leading to the introduction of Intelligent Letter Sorting Machines throughout the country meant that much larger sorting offices requiring larger and larger quantities of mail to make them economically viable became a necessity. This, combined with a decision by British Rail to open a new freight terminal in Willesden, thus removing the need for freight and mail traffic on all of London's main-line stations, contributed to a dramatic reduction in the volumes of post on Mail Rail.

Alongside this, in the 1980s, a comprehensive and increasing network of motorways throughout the United Kingdom made transportation of mail by road in articulated lorries a far more attractive proposition. An ever-growing network of high-speed motorways now connect every major city and carry far more modern and technically advanced vehicles. The age of driverless, fully electric vehicles is fast approaching.

The new model for mail distribution is known as The Mail Centre Rationalisation Programme. It involves the use of large regional mail centres, normally located on the outskirts of large towns and close to good motorway connections, each with its own local collection and distribution network.

In March 2016 Ofcom produced a report entitled: 'Review of the Projected Costs within Royal Mail's Business Plan' that goes some way to justifying the need for this new way of working.

2.3.2 Mail Centre Rationalisation

The modernisation (including the introduction of new machines and the upgrading of existing machines at mail centres and delivery offices) and consolidation of mail centres is one of the core elements of Royal Mail's transformation programme. The number of mail centres was reduced from 69 before the transformation programme to 39 in FYE 2015 (Financial Year Ending) with operations moving from the closed mail centres to other sites. The closed mail centres have been put to new uses, including becoming larger delivery offices or have been disposed of. Royal Mail has also opened four new mail centres. The use of new, or substantially reconfigured, premises for mail centre operations means that sites can be designed specifically to handle parcels and letters rather than older and less suitable sites.

The projects related to 'MC rationalisation' present the finalisation of a process started in FYE 2009. The plan is to finalise ongoing rationalisations and to close two additional mail centres in Portsmouth and Ipswich. The total number of mail centres will then be 37 by the end of FYE 2018.

In 1996 mail and freight was removed from all London main-line stations and the mail was transferred to the Willesden sorting depot, from where mail trains and the remaining travelling post offices departed.

In 2002 only four stations on the line remained open, the Eastern District Office at Whitechapel, Mount Pleasant, the Western District Office at Rathbone Place and Paddington. Consequently on 31st May 2003, the last train ran on the system and Mail Rail was no more.

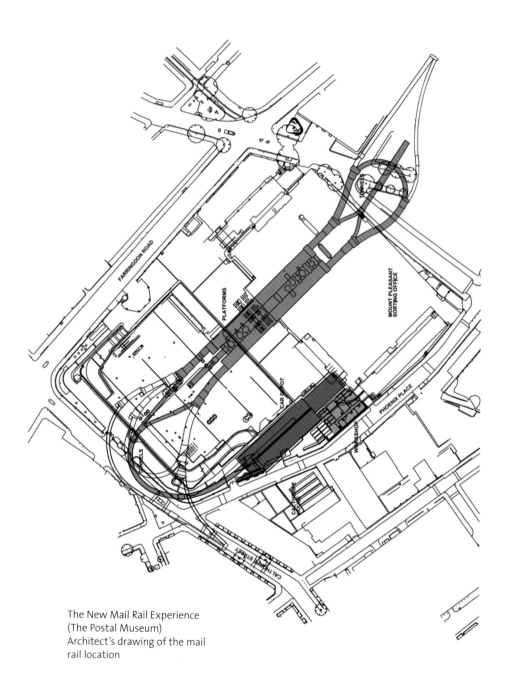

The New Mail Rail Experience
(The Postal Museum)
Architect's drawing of the mail
rail location

The New Beginning

Although the service had stopped, the tunnels and tracks were not abandoned. The system was effectively 'mothballed,' with a small team of maintenance engineers ensuring that the system could be reinstated at short notice if required.

In the ensuing period a number of schemes were considered to make use of the existing tunnels. One scheme was a cycle super highway. Cycling through the 7-foot tunnels up and down a gradient of 1:20 could have proved extremely dangerous and the scheme was not pursued. A proposal for a mushroom farm due to the conditions of the extremely dark tunnels was among other schemes considered but ultimately rejected.

In 2004 the British Postal Heritage Trust was formed to take over the Royal Mail archive. It later became known as The British Postal Museum and Archive, and, most recently, The Postal Museum. After consultations with Royal Mail it was agreed that part of the existing system underneath Mount Pleasant sorting office would be developed as an attraction to tell the story of Mail Rail and provide a ride for its visitors.

The trains, when built, would have to run on a narrow-gauge track through 7-foot tunnels and have to navigate some very tight bends. The original system was not built to, and was never intended to carry passengers. To maximise the space available the third rail running down the centre of the track was removed. A plywood 'mule' was built and pulled around the proposed route to test and attempt to maximise the space available to visitors. At times, the new trains move within an inch of the existing tunnel walls.

Mule used to establish new train dimensions (The Postal Museum)
After calculations based on the mule results the new train goes within an inch of the existing tunnel walls.

Two new trains, one red and one green, to reflect the red Mail Rail trains and the green Post Office Railway trains, were built by Severn Lamb in Alcester. The trains consist of two passenger-carrying coaches each capable of carrying twelve passengers, a driver's control cabin at each end, and one central battery carriage with capacity for eight more passengers.

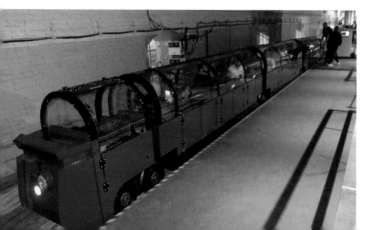

New train (The Postal Museum)

En route on the Mail Rail Ride (The Postal Museum)
The train can carry a maximum of 32 visitors but this
number is seldom reached.

The trains are powered by 24, 6-volt gel batteries connected in
series-parallel to give a 72-volt DC power supply that drives four
24-volt motors, one on each of the four bogies and are controlled
by a programmable controller. The maximum speed of the
trains is approximately 8 miles per hour.

With the restrictions of the narrow gauge, small tunnels and
tight curves the space inside the cabins is tight and the maximum
capacity of 32 passengers is seldom reached.

The Mail Rail exhibition and train ride opened to the public on
4th September 2017. It is open seven days a week and provides a
two-train service at weekends and during school holidays. At
the time of writing a one-train service is provided on weekdays
during term time. As the popularity of the museum increases, it
remains to be seen if a 2-train service will be required on every
day of operation.

Each train does three journeys every hour so the journey time is approximately twenty minutes. For most of the journey through the tunnels there is an audio commentary telling the story of Mail Rail and in each platform a visual presentation shows more.

On leaving the train you return to the Car Depot where larger items of the museum's collections are displayed, including an example of every type of train used on the system since 1927.

There are also exhibits relating to the Pneumatic Tube that preceded the railway, and the Travelling Post Office as well as a number of interactive displays where visitors can explore in more detail how the system worked.

After nearly 80 years of providing a unique and unrivalled service to the Royal Mail and having carried billions of letters and parcels across London, this marvel of Edwardian engineering and ingenuity lives on to educate and entertain future generations.

The Specification for the new trains can be found in Appendix 3.

Appendices

APPENDIX 1

Below is an extract from the Post Office archive describing the history of the post office railway between 1854 and 2003.

- Held at: GB 813 The Royal Mail Archive, Calthorpe House
- Finding Number: POST 20 Series
- Date: 1854-2003
- Level: Series
- Extent: 1 box, 155 files, 35 volumes, 244 plans, 4 sheets, 1 folder, 2 photograph albums.
- Creator Name: GPO
- Administrative or Biographical History:
- The Post Office (London) Railway was opened for traffic in December 1927. The Post Office first showed an interest in using underground railways to transport mail beneath London in 1854 and in 1893 serious consideration was given to running an electric railway in the pneumatic tunnels. By the turn of the twentieth century, traffic congestion in London had reached the point that cross-London journeys by road took so long that an unnecessary number of vehicles had to be used to carry the ever growing volume of mails between sorting offices and main line termini. In 1905, the Metropolitan Pneumatic Despatch Co presented a bill to Parliament for the construction of a pneumatic line connecting the major railway termini and Post Offices. The Bill was rejected as being too ambitious. In September 1909 the Postmaster General appointed a Committee to examine the practicality of the transmission of mails in London by pneumatic tube or electric railway. The Committee reported in February 1911 in favour of an electric railway

between Paddington Station (Great Western Railway) and the Eastern District Post Office in Whitechapel Road, a distance of six and a half miles. The scheme was submitted by the Postmaster General to the Cabinet in 1912 and power to construct the railway was given to the Postmaster General by the Post Office (London) Railway Act, 1913. The Act made provision for compensation for damage and allowed the Post Office a budget of £1,100,000 to construct the line with stations at Paddington, Western District Office, Western Parcel Office, West Central District Office, Mount Pleasant Sorting Office, King Edward Building, Liverpool Street and East District Office. Tenders for the construction of the tunnel were invited on the 26 August 1914. John Mowlem and Co. won the tender to construct the tunnels and build eight stations. The work, although interrupted by the war, was completed in 1917. In parallel with the building work, Post Office engineers built a test track on Plumstead Marshes to experiment with the control systems and rolling stock. However, the war caused the testing to be brought to a premature halt. During the war the stations became a home for exhibits from museums. The cessation of the war enabled the Post Office to proceed with their plans, and in 1919 tenders were issued for the supply and installation of the electrical equipment. Prices proved too expensive for the post war budget and the scheme was held in abeyance until 1923 when tenders were reissued.

In May 1927, work was sufficiently advanced for half the system to be handed over for staff training and in December of that year the scheme received Parliamentary approval and the line became fully operational with parcels traffic running between Mount Pleasant and Paddington. Mount Pleasant to Liverpool Street opened for Christmas parcels from 19-24 December and then for a full parcels service from 28 December. Liverpool Street to Eastern District Office opened for parcels on 2 January

1928. Letter traffic began on 13 February with the opening of West Central District Office station, followed by Western District Office on 12 March. The line proved an immense benefit to the Post Office in the first year of operation, however the high mileage gave the Post Office problems as the cars needed a lot of maintenance. In the early 1930s the rolling stock underwent a gradual change as the cars were replaced by three car trains. These trains were replaced by 34 new trains in 1981 in a £1 million development programme.

In a Press Release, issued by the Post Office PR team on 7 November 2002, Royal Mail announced that unless it could find a new backer, that the Post Office underground railway would close in the near future. The working operation finally ceased on 30 May 2003, but the system has in fact been 'mothballed' in the hope that an alternative use can be found for it.

- Description: This series relates to the conveyance of mails by Underground pneumatic tube in London. It comprises reports and papers produced and used by the committee appointed in 1909 by the Postmaster General to consider the introduction of the underground transmission of mails within London and plans of the proposed route for the railway, showing rail levels and junctions. It also contains a copy of the Post Office (London) Railway act and the patent granted to Hosiah Latimer Clark for the invention of apparatus for conveying post by pneumatic tube, (POST 20/30). Papers relating to the construction, maintenance and expansion of the Post Office (London) Railway are also present including specifications, invitations to tender, conditions of contract, estimate of costs and technical plans relating to the construction of new stations, car depots, subways, additions and alterations to stations, including the fitting and maintenance of electrical equipment. This is also demonstrated through numerous plans held within the collection. As well as the Manager's annual reports, there are also numerous files of miscellaneous correspondence, memoranda and reports from the Post Office to various departments and organisations regarding the Post Office (London) Railway, historical accounts. There are also two photograph albums of railway equipment and work being carried out on it.

Some of the plans show properties purchased by the Post Office following the passage of the Post Office (London) Railway Act in 1913. There is a series of signed plans dated 26 October 1914 showing the depth and route of the Post Office (London) railway below ground with details of tunnels, shield chambers, and shafts. There is also a series of plans marking individual and corporate properties along the proposed route of the Post Office Railway.

Appendix 2

Stock List

This list shows the works numbers of the units as delivered new to the Post Office Railway. The number (in brackets) is the recent number, this giving an idea of stock that was last in service on the system. Although not carrying a modern number, some disused stock was stored in various sidings around the system.

1926 English Electric Battery Locos. Only 3 built.

1 (1)	2 (2)	3 (3)			

1927 English Electric units. 90 built.

591	592	593	594	595	596
597	598	599	600	601	602
603	604	605	606	607	608
609	610	611	612	613	614
615	616	617	618	619	620
621	622	623	624	625	626
627	628	629	630	631	632
633	634	635	636	637	638
639	640	641	642	643	644
645	646	647	648	649	650
651	652	653	654	655	656

657	658	659	660	661	662
663	664	665	666	667	668
669	670	671	672	673	674
675	676	677	678	679	680

1930/31 English Electric articulated units. 50 built.

First Batch, delivered up to May 1930.

752	753	754	755 (35)	756 (36)	757
758	759	760 (37)	761 (38)	762 (39)	763

Second Batch, delivered from Sept 1930.

793	794	795	796	797	798
799	800	801 (40)	802	803	804
805 (41)	806 (42)	807	808	809	810
811 (43)	812 (44)	813	814 (45)	815 (46)	816
817	818	819 (47)	820	821	822
823	824 (48)	825	826	827 (49)	828
829	830				

1936 English Electric articulated units.

923	924	925	926	927	928 (50)
929	930	931 (51)	932		

1962 English Electric prototype units. Only 2 built.

1	2 (66)				

1980 Greenbat units. 35 built.

501 (01)	502 (02)	503 (03)	504 (04)	505 (05)	506 (06)
507 (07)	508 (08)	509 (09)	510 (10)	511 (11)	512 (12)
513 (13)	514 (14)	515 (15)	516 (16)	517 (17)	518 (18)
519 (19)	520 (20)	521 (21)	522 (22)	523 (23)	524 (24)
525 (25)	526 (26)	527 (27)	528 (28)	529 (29)	530 (30)
531 (31)	532 (32)	533 (33)	534 (34)	535 ()	

In addition, the following cars are preserved:

601: Mount Pleasant workshop – 1927 4-wheel stock

803: Buckingham Railway Centre, Quainton Road.1930/1 English Electric

807: Science Museum (stored) – 1930/1 English Electric

808: Chalk Pits Museum, Amberly – 1930/1 English Electric

809: National Railway Museum, York, – 1930/1 English Electric

APPENDIX 3

Severn Lamb Train Specification

The table below summarises the technical details of the train:

Specification	Description
Vehicle Type	Passenger Carrying Rail Vehicle
Drive System	Battery Electric
Minimum track radius	16m
Maximum track gradient	5% for 210m
Maximum operating speed	10.5kph (6.5mph)
Normal Operating Speed	7.2kph (4.5mph)
Rail Type	BS35 (Original Rail Specification) and BS35M (Replacement Rail Specification)
Motor Power	4Kw Nominal 6Kw Peak. Total Vehicle Installed Power is 16Kw Nominal 24Kw Peak.
Battery Specification	72 Volt Battery Pack consisting of 24 off 6 Volt AGM Gel Type Cells Connected in a Series Parallel Configuration. Battery Capacity is 840 Ah at the 20 hour rate.

Train Dimensions	
Wheel arrangement	4 off 4 wheel power bogies
Gauge	610mm (24")
Train Dimensions	16348mm long x 946mm wide x 1492mm tall
Train Net Weight	6884 kg
Train Gross Weight	9604 kg
Coaches	
No. Coaches	3
Passenger Coach capacity	24 passengers (Adult/Child mix)
Battery Car Passenger Capacity	8 passengers (Adult/Child) mix
Coach Style	Fully enclosed
Passenger Weight	80 kg
Environmental	
Operating temperatures	5° C to 30° C
Humidity	50%
Altitude	Vehicle Operational Below Ground Level

Further Reading

There are three main volumes that describe the construction and operation of the Post Office Railway. All are now hard to obtain but may be viewed by appointment at the British Library or the Postal Museum.

'The Post Office Tube Railway London'. Reprinted from *Engineering* (issues of 27th January, 10th and 24th February, and 2nd and 16th March 1928), London 1928.

Major W. G. Carter M.C., 'The Post Office (London) Railway'. Post Office Green Paper No 36. General Post Office, 1937.

Derek A. Bayliss, 'The Post Office Railway London'. Turntable Publications, Sheffield, 1978.

Other sources referred to in the preparation of this book were:

Mailrail.co.uk: unofficial website of the Post Office Railway.

'Mail Rail Manual'. The Postal Museum, 2017.

Peter Johnson, 'Mail by Rail. The history of the TPO and Post Office Railway'. 1995.

'Mike's Railway History Driverless Subway Trains'. http://mikes.railhistory.railfan.net/r023.html

A. C. Mackay, 'The new Post Office Railway Station at the New Western District Office'.

'Post Office Railway – Change to Mercury Arc Rectifiers' *P.O.E.E.J.* vol. 52 p.300 Jan 1960.

'The Story of Mail Rail'. Postalmuseum.org.

'Mail Rail a photographic Exhibition'. The British Postal Museum & Archive.

Heritage Trust award granted to the Museum in 2018

Author Biography

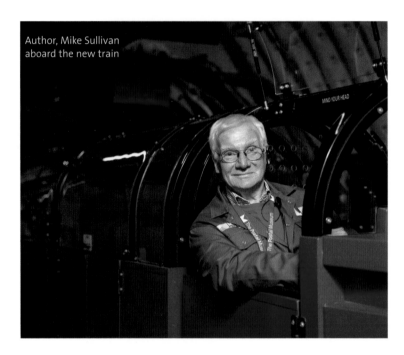

Author, Mike Sullivan aboard the new train

Mike started his working life as a 'Youth in Training' on the Post Office Railway in January 1962. After this intensive training period he became a technician on the railway and, after a further year's training, a Technical Officer. He obtained a City and Guilds Full Technician's Certificate with endorsements, a Higher National Certificate with endorsements and a degree from the Open University.

After spells on research at Dollis Hill and Martlesham and on Postal Mechanisation in Southampton he left the General Post Office in August 1976. He then worked as an Electrical Supervisor at a fully automated food processing plant before going to Africa as a Contracts Manager giving electricity to eight small towns that had never had it before.

On his return he did a Master's Degree in Industrial Management with a thesis on Robotics and continued as an independent consultant, mainly managing large computer infrastructure projects.

Mike retired from Fujitsu as a Senior Project Manager in 2010. He returned to the railway when it opened as part of the Postal Museum in September 2017 and now works on a part-time basis as a driver/operator.